3/98

6 x 10/08

★ SPORTS STARS ★

KENNY LOFTON
MAN OF STEAL

BY MARK STEWART

Children's Press®

A Division of Grolier Publishing
New York London Hong Kong Sydney
Danbury, Connecticut

Photo Credits
©: Allsport USA: 22, 28 (Stephen Dunn); AP/Wide World Photos: 13 right,
41; John Klein: 17, 26, 33; Mel Bailey: 27; Robert A. Walker: 21, 44 top right;
Ron Vesely: 36, 45 top left; Sports Illustrated Picture Collection: 18, 44 top
left (Peter Read Miller), 10 (Dr. David Walberg); SportsChrome East/West: 9
(Louis A. Raynor), 14, 31, 32, 35, 38 (Rob Tringali Jr.); Tom Dipace: 3, 7, 43,
45 top right, 46, 47; UPI/Corbis-Bettmann: 13 left.

Library of Congress Cataloging-in-Publication Data

Stewart, Mark.
    Kenny Lofton: man of steal / by Mark Stewart.
      p. cm. - (Sports stars)
      Summary: A biography of the base-stealing outfielder for the
    Cleveland Indians who has won four Golden Gloves in his first five
    seasons as a major league player.
      ISBN 0-516-20488-2 (lib. bdg.)   0-516-26053-7 (pbk.)
      1. Lofton, Kenny, 1967–   –Juvenile literature. 2. Baseball players–
    United States–Biography–Juvenile literature. [1. Lofton, Kenny,
    1967– . 2. Baseball players. 3. Afro-Americans–Biography.]
      I. Title. II. Series.
GV865.l64S84 1998
796.357'092   96-50988
[B]-DC21   CIP
                                        AC

★ CONTENTS ★

★ 1 ★

THE MASTER OF THE STEAL

From first base, Kenny Lofton concentrates on the opposing pitcher's movements. Kenny takes a safe lead and waits. The pitcher checks on Kenny briefly before firing the ball to the plate. "Strike!" calls the umpire. The catcher returns the ball to the pitcher. None of the pitcher's moves surprise Kenny. For the past week, he has carefully studied the pitcher in game films and printed reports. He knows all the pitcher's pickoff moves and gestures. Kenny looks at second base and takes a long lead. The

pitcher checks on him again. Kenny's legs tighten as he waits for the precise moment . . . NOW! Kenny explodes into speed as the pitcher completes his delivery. The catcher frantically throws to second base—but it is too late. Kenny slides in safely and calls for time. The catcher shakes his head, worried that Kenny might try to steal third!

★ 2 ★

AGAINST THE ODDS

Kenny learned many tough lessons on the streets of East Chicago.

East Chicago, Indiana, is like many midwestern cities. There are factories and stores. There are parks and playgrounds. There are rich people and poor people. And there are good parts and bad parts. Kenny Lofton grew up on the tough side of town, where street crime and drugs were a constant threat and families struggled to

Kenny's grandmother insisted that he follow her rules as he was growing up.

make ends meet. Some would say that the odds were against Kenny from the start: his mother was just 14 years old when he was born, and he never knew his father. It was left to Kenny's grandmother, Rosie Person, to raise the boy.

It was not easy. Putting food on the table was often a challenge for Rosie, and the apartment they shared had cold, concrete floors and cracked windows. It was hot in the summer and cold in the winter. Kenny was used to doing without. "We were very poor," he remembers. "I wanted a lot of things, but we couldn't afford them."

Kenny's grandmother had four important rules: Do your homework when you get home from school. Pay attention in class. Choose your heroes wisely. And root for the Chicago Cubs with all your heart. For the most part, Kenny followed these rules. "Basically, you had to get your homework done before dinner," he says. "Math was my favorite subject growing up. I enjoyed working with numbers. My least favorite subject was history. I couldn't understand why we were going over something that happened 200 years ago. I thought it was better to worry about what was wrong in today's society. I guess I dealt with the fact I didn't like it by just 'swallowing the pill' and working hard. I had no choice."

One thing Kenny did have a choice about was reading. He hoped to be a police officer one day, and he knew that reading well would help him succeed. "Developing good reading skills is very important, probably the most important thing you'll do," Kenny says. "You use those skills your entire life and it makes things a lot easier if you have good reading skills. Reading is something you should never take for granted."

Kenny's heroes were Rosa Parks and Jackie Robinson. In 1955, Parks became one of the key figures in the civil rights movement when she refused to give up her bus seat to a white person

Kenny's heroes are Rosa Parks (above, left) and Jackie Robinson (above, right).

in Montgomery, Alabama. In 1947, Robinson broke baseball's "color barrier" when he became the first African-American in the major leagues.

For Kenny, baseball demands more thought than basketball.

The big sport in Kenny's neighborhood was not baseball, however. It was basketball. And eventually, he began to join in the games at the local playground. "But baseball was my first love," he says. "I didn't even start playing basketball until the sixth grade. Baseball is a harder game than basketball, but it's more enjoyable. In baseball, you have to anticipate what's coming next. You're thinking all the time."

Kenny enrolled at Washington High School in 1981 and made the baseball team as a freshman the following spring. He started all four years, and performed well enough as a pitcher and outfielder to attract the interest of some pro and college teams. Ironically, the scouts were scared away by Kenny's success on the basketball court.

Kenny joined the Washington High hoops squad as a junior and immediately became the team's biggest star. Although he stood just 5' 10", he could take the ball to the hole and jam over taller forwards and centers. Kenny was also a great passer and a great defender. He earned all-state honors as a senior and was recruited by several top colleges. He eventually decided to attend the University of Arizona.

Looking back, Kenny realizes he probably should have gone directly into baseball. But no schools offered him a baseball scholarship. And no major-league team would waste a draft pick on a young man who seemed bound for stardom in another sport.

"I guess I got caught up in the hype in basketball, and I didn't think about baseball like I should have," Kenny admits. "Growing up, people would tell me baseball was going to be my future, because my height and speed and things I do are geared toward baseball. But people tell you things and you don't really listen."

Later, Kenny would admit that he should have concentrated on baseball earlier.

During his first years at the University of Arizona, Kenny devoted himself to basketball.

★ 3 ★

FROM BASKETBALL
TO BASEBALL

Kenny Lofton was one of three promising freshmen recruited by Arizona coach Lute Olsen. At first, Kenny thought about playing both basketball and baseball, but basketball practice alone barely left time for his studies. Besides, Arizona's baseball team had won the national championship two years earlier, so he knew he could not just show up and expect to play. Even as a basketball player, Kenny sat on the bench for most of his first year and served mainly as a defensive substitution.

During his sophomore year, Kenny started for the basketball team and set a school record for steals, with 55. The following year, in the 1988 NCAA Tournament, Arizona made it all the way to the Final Four before losing to Oklahoma University. After the tournament, Kenny began to think about baseball again. "I really started to miss baseball. I just wanted to get the feel of swinging the bat again."

That April, he joined the Arizona junior varsity baseball team as an outfielder, and he even appeared in five games for the varsity team, primarily as a pinch-runner. Kenny's big break came when Clark Crist, a Houston Astros scout who had played college ball at Arizona, returned to the campus to look over the team's new players. He liked what he saw in Kenny and told him that he had a future in baseball. The Astros drafted Kenny in the 17th round of the next amateur draft and offered him a minor-league contract. They were willing to teach him the game, if he was willing to learn.

Despite his basketball skills, Kenny could not resist playing for the Arizona baseball team.

With the Astros organization, Kenny learned to take advantage of his speed.

For the second time in his young life, Kenny was being asked to choose between baseball and basketball. Kenny asked his grandmother for advice. "I looked at both situations, talked to my grandmother, and did what I thought was best for me," he recalls. "She just told me to go back and get my degree."

Kenny signed with the Astros on two conditions: that he could return to Arizona for his senior year and continue practicing basketball while he played baseball. Kenny played pro baseball for Auburn of the New York–Penn League during the summer of 1988. He batted just .214, but no one worried about the low average, because he was learning a new way to hit. "They adjusted my swing so I could hit the ball into the ground— they wanted me to take advantage of my speed," he says of the coaches. Also, he had to adjust to using a wooden bat because he had only used aluminum bats in college.

Kenny finished up the spring semester and received his degree in communications. He was still undecided about which sport to pursue, and he waited anxiously to see whether he would be selected in the NBA's June draft. When his name was not called, he felt the decision had been made for him. "That's when I started thinking baseball," he says. "I realized it was going to be my career. My first year, my mind was on two sports. But after that, I was concentrating totally on baseball. My mind was where it needed to be."

★ 4 ★

JOURNEY TO
THE MAJOR LEAGUES

Kenny Lofton returned to Auburn for his
second year of professional baseball. In
34 games, he hit .264 and stole 26 bases. After
being promoted to Asheville of the South
Atlantic League, he hit .329 and racked up 14
more steals. He was also starting to do the little
things that spell the difference between success
and failure: getting better jumps on fly balls;
reading the moves of pitchers; recognizing the
spin on pitches; throwing to the right base; and
bunting for hits. Kenny was beginning to get the
feel of the game again.

Kenny's attention to detail in the minor leagues allowed him to grow into a major leaguer.

"After my second year, I felt pretty comfortable," he says. "I started to pick it back up. The reaction part was tough. Seeing the ball. Hitting the ball. The toughest pitch to hit is the off-speed pitch. If you have good hand-eye coordination, it will work out. But it's still pretty tough. People don't understand how long it takes to get to the level you want to be. The longer you wait to do something, the longer it takes you to get back."

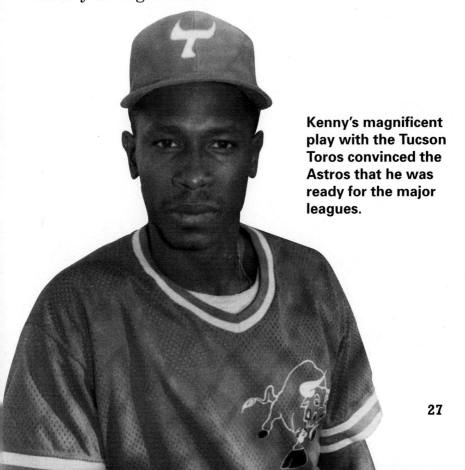

Kenny's magnificent play with the Tucson Toros convinced the Astros that he was ready for the major leagues.

Because the Astros were in last place, Kenny got a lot of playing time when he was first called up.

By 1990, Kenny was definitely back on the fast track. He finished second in the Florida State League in batting average, runs, and stolen bases, while leading the league in hits. In 1991, he was promoted all the way to Triple-A. Playing for the Tucson Toros, he topped the Pacific Coast League (PCL) in hits and had more triples than anyone else in baseball. Kenny was voted the PCL's top prospect and was voted Most Valuable Player in the league's championship series. He led the Toros to their first title in 23 years with a .450 batting average.

As a reward for his fine performance, Kenny was called up by the Astros a few days later. The team was in last place, so he got a chance to play almost every day. In 20 games, he batted just .203 and stole only 2 bases. Nevertheless, he convinced most baseball people that he was ready to play in the majors. He played hard all the time and never seemed overmatched or intimidated.

The Astros liked what they saw, but they decided that Kenny could be traded. Houston needed a catcher badly, so they traded Kenny to the Cleveland Indians for a young backstop named Ed Taubensee and pitcher Willie Blair. "The Astros traded me to the right situation, and I thank them for that," says Kenny. "I was going from one last-place team to another, but I was getting an opportunity to play. That's all I wanted."

Within two seasons, Houston fans were calling the trade the worst deal in 25 years. Kenny won the Indians' starting center field job in the spring of 1992, and by the end of the season he broke the American League record for steals by a rookie, with 66. Also, Kenny walked more than he struck out—a great accomplishment for a young lead-off hitter in his first full big-league season. And he showed his toughness by doing this with a fractured bone in his left hand during the final three months.

After arriving in Cleveland, Kenny won a spot in the starting lineup.

As a hitter, Kenny was very selective and rarely swung at bad pitches.

In the outfield, Kenny gunned down 14 runners, defying reports that he had a weak arm. Little did the scouts know that he had been building up his arm strength and accuracy with a regular long-throwing routine!

In center field, Kenny became a better defensive player by building up his arm strength.

★ ★ ★

Kenny's second season with the Indians was marred by a tragic accident that occurred in spring training. Two of his teammates were killed and another seriously injured when their powerboat slammed into a dock. The team was down all season long and finished 10 games below .500. Kenny, however, continued to play well. He led the league with 70 stolen bases, batted .325, and scored 116 runs.

Before the 1994 season began, Kenny sensed that the team still needed a lift. So in spring training, he turned the Cleveland clubhouse into his own personal playground. He played practical jokes on his teammates and kept the Indians loose with his good-natured ribbing of veterans Carlos Baerga and Albert Belle. In his own special way, Kenny was becoming a team leader. The club was having its best record in decades, and Kenny was leading the American League in hits and steals when a labor dispute ended the season after only 113 games.

By the end of the 1993 season, Kenny's hitting and baserunning had become an important part of the Cleveland offense.

In 1994, Kenny became an important leader for the Indians.

Kenny was starting to gain recognition as one of baseball's top offensive weapons. In his mind, though, it was his defense that was winning ball games. "I know you get recognition in this game by what you do offensively," he says. "Nobody ever talks about defense or puts the focus on it like they probably should. I've always enjoyed playing defense. It was that way when I played basketball—defense was always my specialty. On defense, I can control people's minds by catching the ball. The opposing team gets frustrated, and it also helps the pitcher out. You make a catch— he'll feel more confident throwing that pitch again."

**Kenny and the Indians had high expectations for the
1995 season.**

⭐ 5 ⭐

TO THE WORLD SERIES

Cleveland fans could hardly wait for the
1995 season to begin. For the first time
since the 1950s, the team was favored to win
the American League pennant. Kenny had
another good year, despite injuries to his back,
ribs, and hamstring. In the final 29 games, he
swiped 22 bases to win his third consecutive
stolen-base crown. And the Indians won 100
games and made it to the American League
Championship Series. There, they battled the
Seattle Mariners for the right to play the
National League champion in the World Series.

With the teams tied at two games each and the series headed back to Seattle for Games Six and Seven, the Indians had to win Game Five. The Mariners broke a 1–1 tie in the fifth inning when Albert Belle waved off Kenny on a pop fly and then failed to make the catch. Cleveland scored two runs to regain the lead, but with two outs in the ninth, Seattle's Edgar Martinez lined a ball to the wall in right-center. It looked like a sure double until Kenny flashed into the gap and snared it to end the game.

In Game Six, Kenny scored all the way from second base on a passed ball to seal Seattle's fate. The Indians won 4–0 to capture their first pennant since 1954. In just four years, Kenny had helped the Indians go from last place to the World Series!

The Indians lost the 1995 World Series to the Atlanta Braves, but Kenny led all players with six runs scored. And in Game Three, he put on an unforgettable show. He collected three hits

Kenny is mobbed by his teammates after beating Seattle in the playoffs.

and three walks and scored three times in a thrilling 11-inning victory.

Just before the 1997 season, Kenny was stunned to learn that he was traded to the Atlanta Braves. The Indians feared that Kenny would leave the team when he became a free agent in 1998, so they decided to trade Kenny while they still could get players in return. Cleveland traded Kenny and pitcher Allan Embree to Atlanta for All-Star outfielders David Justice and Marquis Grissolm.

Starting in a new city in a new league is tough for any ball player. But Kenny displayed his talent and quickly established himself as the main man in the Braves' lineup. With a trophy case full of Gold Gloves and stolen-base crowns, Kenny has little left to prove on the ball field. But until he and his teammates can call themselves world champions, he will never stop looking for ways to win. That, of course, is what makes Kenny Lofton one of the best players in baseball.

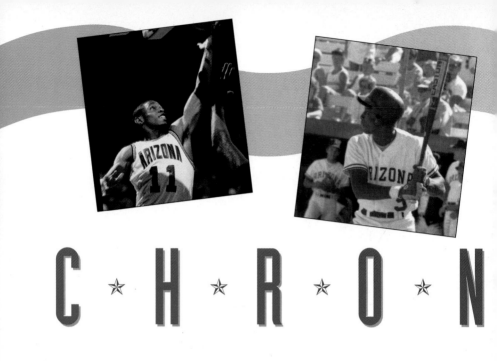

C ⋆ H ⋆ R ⋆ O ⋆ N

1967	• Kenny Lofton is born in East Chicago, Indiana.
1981	• Kenny attends Washington High School, where he plays both basketball and baseball.
1985	• Kenny accepts a basketball scholarship to the University of Arizona.
1988	• Kenny helps the basketball team reach the NCAA Final Four. After basketball season, Kenny joins the junior-varsity baseball team. He is noticed by Clark Crist, who offers Kenny a Houston Astros minor-league contract. Kenny accepts and plays pro baseball that summer in the New York–Penn League.
1989	• Kenny is not selected by the NBA draft, and he decides to concentrate on baseball. He returns to play in the New York–Penn League and is soon promoted to the South Atlantic League.
1990	• Kenny is promoted to the Florida State League, and he continues to play well.

O ★ L ★ O ★ G ★ Y

1991 • After impressing the Houston coaches, Kenny plays Triple-A baseball for the Tucson Toros. The Houston Astros call up Kenny after he has a great season.

1992 • Houston trades Kenny to the Cleveland Indians at the beginning of the year. Kenny breaks the rookie record for base stealing and finishes second in Rookie-of-the-Year voting.

1993 • Despite Cleveland's poor performance, Kenny steals 70 bases, bats .325, and scores 116 runs.

1994 • Kenny leads the American League with 160 base hits until a labor dispute ends the baseball season.

1995 • Kenny leads the Indians to the American League pennant and the World Series, where they are defeated by the Atlanta Braves.

1997 • Kenny is traded to the Atlanta Braves.

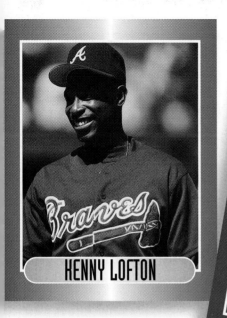

KENNY LOFTON

KENNY LOFTON

Place of Birth East Chicago, Indiana

Date of Birth May 31, 1967

Height 6′ 0″

Weight 180 pounds

High School Washington High School

College University of Arizona

Pro Teams Houston Astros, Cleveland Indians, Atlanta Braves

Honors Rookie Base-Stealing Record

★ MAJOR LEAGUE STATISTICS ★

Season	Team	Hits	Doubles	Triples	Runs	Avg.	Stolen Bases
1991	Houston	15	1	0	9	.203	2
1992	Cleveland	164	15	8	96	.285	66*
1993	Cleveland	185	28	8	116	.325	70*
1994	Cleveland	160*	32	9	105	.349	60*
1995	Cleveland	149	22	13*	93	.310	54*
1996	Cleveland	210	35	4	132	.317	75*
Totals		**883**	**133**	**42**	**551**	**.313**	**327**

*Led league

ABOUT THE AUTHOR

Mark Stewart grew up in New York City in the 1960s and 1970s—when the Mets, Jets, and Knicks all had championship teams. As a child, Mark read everything about sports he could lay his hands on. Today, he is one of the busiest sportswriters around. Since 1990, he has written close to 500 sports stories for kids, including profiles on more than 200 athletes, past and present. A graduate of Duke University, Mark served as senior editor of *Racquet,* a national tennis magazine, and was managing editor of *Super News*, a sporting goods industry newspaper. He is the author of every Grolier All-Pro Biography and eight titles in the Sports Stars series.